THE RIGHT STORY LEADS TO SUCCESS

A Guide to Business Storytelling

By

Kieron P. Chambers

© **Copyright 2019**

All rights reserved.

This report is towards furnishing precise and solid data concerning the point and issue secured. The production is sold with the possibility that the distributor isn't required to render bookkeeping, formally allowed, or something else, qualified administrations. On the off chance that exhortation is important, lawful, or proficient, a rehearsed individual in the calling ought to be requested.

The Declaration of Principles, which was also recognized and endorsed by the Committee of the American Bar Association and the Committee of Publishers and Associations.

Not the slightest bit is it lawful to replicate, copy, or transmit any piece of this report in either electronic methods or the printed group. Recording of this distribution is carefully disallowed, and any capacity of this report isn't permitted except if with composed authorization from the distributor. All rights held.

The data gave in this is expressed, to be honest, and predictable, in that any risk, as far as absentmindedness or something else, by any utilization or maltreatment of any approaches, procedures, or bearings contained inside is the singular and articulate obligation of the beneficiary peruser. By no means will any lawful obligation or fault be held against the distributor for any reparation, harms, or money related misfortune because of the data in this, either straightforwardly or by implication.

Particular creators claim all copyrights not held by the distributor.

The data in this is offered for educational purposes exclusively and is all-inclusive as so. The introduction of the data is without a contract or any sort of assurance confirmation.

The trademarks that are utilized are with no assent, and the distribution of the trademark is without consent or support by the trademark proprietor. All trademarks and brands inside this book are for explaining purposes just and are simply possessed by the proprietors, not partnered with this record.

TABLE OF CONTENTS

INTRODUCTION 5
WHAT ARE BUSINESS STORIES 6
BASICS OF BUSINESS STORIES. 10
ELEMENTS OF STORYTELLING 15
COMPLEX BUT CLEAR 25
USE OWN STORIES TO BUILD CREDIBILITY 38
STORY HOOKS 41
THE SECRET STRATEGY THAT MASTER STORYTELLERS USE. 44
HOW TO ENGAGE YOUR AUDIENCE 50
CONCLUSION 60

INTRODUCTION

The organisation plays a major function within our culture. It is a competitive and innovative task that continuously adds to the shaping of our culture. By satisfying the needs and wants individuals can not please themselves, businesses enhance the quality of life for people and also create a higher standard of living.

It is a means for individuals to offer items and services to consumers, and at the exact same time, create a profit on their own. Businesses are not just crucial since they offer products and also services to customers. However, they also boost the economy as well as boost jobs for individuals within society which is an extra truth producing a greater standard of life.

Modern technology executes an essential component in one of the essential variables indicated for the hospitality market guest satisfaction. You require the newest in innovation to regulate your resort's procedures as well as the picked supplier has to be effective and also respected on the market as well as ought to offer definitely cost-free breakthroughs. Additionally, it's vital to recognise brand-new innovation that individuals are making use of daily that may change the process section.

WHAT ARE BUSINESS STORY

Evidently, inside our brains, we have 'tale themes' prepared and waiting to place the details we obtain. If this information is presented in a tale style, it sticks much better. Usually, they aren't seen as stories; they are sometimes simply scenarios repainted or genuine life instances that we determine with.

Advertising and marketing isn't a blunt instrument that paints all customers the exact same or that sees everyone similarly as your potential consumer. I listen to 'everyone is my consumer' fairly a whole lot from customers when I initially meet them. You require to understand this in order to craft your story.

In the stories a company tells-- be it on a site, promotional brochure or sales email-- clients require to identify with the trouble being fixed. They require to see themselves as the consumer you explain, as the person that requires that exact issue resolved. A lot of service websites set out speaking about their product or services attributes rather than the consumer's trouble. They fall short of influencing and also link activity. They make use of way too much jargon, stumbled upon boring or featureless, or worse audio similar to their competitor. When they do speak about themselves they can do it coldly-- they believe 'expertly'-- however with no actual impact. I'm constantly attempting to obtain clients to place even more of what they are and what their customers are into their interactions. OK, you won't attract everyone, yet that's the point. You appeal better to the consumer you are attempting to bring in. The 'regarding us' area is among the most vital web pages on an internet site. It's one of the most checked out web pages on a web site. You want the possibility to think 'she's like me' or 'I such as that'. 'That's my specific issue' or 'that company is for me'. This is the connection that influences activity.A service device can be thought about as any kind of property that assists or helps the organisation to attain its stated objectives or goals. There are different sorts of devices that might be utilized in a service varying in size, intricacy, value, and threat to the business operation. There are the large, hefty tools such as cooktops, refrigerators, fridges freezer or cars. This system intends to take into consideration the items that are mobile as well as beneficial, and by their actual nature, present unique administration challenges to business. When considering their various other cousins, there are different considerations that relate to the monitoring of these things that are not applicable. It is very easy to lose a mobile telephone, yet extremely difficult to misplace a freezer. The cost of utilizing a cellphone can vary significantly; the cost to the business of the mobile can be affordable or exorbitant relying on usage. It is additionally a difficulty to abuse a freezer. There have been several cases where the abuse of a telephone has actually had considerable implications for staff members and also for the business. Modern managers must be able to take care of these devices to ensure that they are available when required, are in a useful as well as running condition and that the individual is sufficiently educated to use the device efficiently. A cellphone must have an adequately charged battery, a mobile service, and also a customer who is sufficiently educated or experienced to be able to make use of the tool in a productive as well as reliable way.

To continue the instance of the mobile telephone, it is possible to picture a scenario where a staff member is given a phone with a level battery. A charger is at some point located, and the battery charged. When the phone is switched on, it requests a safety and security code, which is unknown, however additionally later situated. When this is entered, it is discovered that the bill has actually not been paid as well as there is no solution. This is a basic example of the care and monitoring that is necessary to guarantee that the device does fulfil the requirements of business and that the tool boosts the performance of a business.

Each company will certainly need to create standards so regarding determining which devices are to be monitored and as a result regulated to make sure that time, as well as initiative, is committed to handling the proper and also crucial devices. Undoubtedly a smartphone supplied to a salesman will require to be kept track of and controlled to make certain that all costs are consistent with company activity. The mobile of the company owner is most likely immune from such controls. A mobile phone might get on a contract and have an acquisition rate of absolutely no, while a stapler to deal with the paper with each other may cost a few hundred dollars.

There are a number of requirements that might be used to categorize an organisation and recognize tool, and a lot of organisations will certainly utilize a mix of these criteria to develop the classification of an individual device.

BASICS OF BUSINESS STORIES

Appropriate discussion of information in the type of graphs or graphs can be a valuable evaluation tool as well as if the information is after that effectively analyzed this can facilitate the decision-making process.Accounting data is often presented in the type of tables of numbers, in some cases simply as a print out from a spreadsheet or records from an accounting software package. While this design of discussion gives detailed figures, it may not constantly be one of the most reliable ways to present and connect information. It may be that some essential info needs to be highlighted, probably connections between specific numbers need to be emphasised, or patterns recognized. Suitable discussion of data in the form of graphs or graphs can be a useful analysis tool as well as if the data is after that properly interpreted, this can facilitate the decision-making process.There is much software that allows the individual to produce charts that look very professional, but it is necessary to think about the various kinds of graphs readily available and also pick an ideal chart kind for the information being presented. Offering data in an unsuitable chart can communicate details which may be deceptive. The term 'chart' is normally taken into consideration to consist of all kinds of charts, and any type of various other sorts of the chart made use of to give a pictorial presentation of the data.

Maintain the story basic yet relatable. You do not need plot spins as well as personality arcs; you require a tale that will resonate with your audience. Straighten your problem with something they've experienced themselves if you're pitching to a customer.

Every fantastic power has inherent risks and rewards in using it, and storytelling in management interaction is no different. Tell the wrong tale in the wrong circumstance, and also you risk of your audience gazing blankly at you, wondering quietly (or worse, out loud) what the factor of your story was and just how they get back the three mins you just extracted from their lives in informing it. Yet share the ideal story in the appropriate situation, and the benefits can be excellent, specifically in your capability to connect with your audience at an extra human degree, and also indirectly shape the method you want them to assume and feel concerning whatever you're collected to existing, review or discuss.

To gain the greatest incentives from storytelling in the office and stay away from the dangers, leaders should believe purposefully concerning the tales they inform, making sure they can first recognize what they require a tale to accomplish so they can after that discover or develop the appropriate tale to accomplish it. It additionally involves building great tales to be told.

Premise

This is the context for your story, linking the tale you are about to tell to the office scenario in which you're informing it as well as the mind-set of the audience who's hearing it. Establishing the facility for your tale is a way of setting it up, developing a usual understanding with your target market and also helping them much better value why they ought to listen to it.

Platform

After you've developed the property for your story, you after that establish the starting point for it by developing the moment and also place in which it begins. "Once upon a time in a galaxy far, much away" is the system for one of the most well-known tales of our time (Star Wars). When a writer sets the platform, it's his or her cue that a story has to do with the unravelling.

Person

Many stories have a major character whom the tale is about, with sustaining characters having an influence on him or her and/or journeying along with them. Fairly usually, the main personality is you, the author, as you share an individual story regarding something that occurred to you and also what you took away from that experience (the point). Sometimes you can inform an individual tale where you are not the main personality.

Plot

While there are numerous plots a tale can follow, the most regular includes a group of individuals (individual) in an existing circumstance (platform) who have a goal of attaining a brand-new truth but experience barriers and challenges in attempting to get to that goal, and then somehow handle to conquer them. A tale's story becomes extra interesting when there is stress constructed up around those challenges as well as challenges, as well as that stress is soothed when the personalities are successful by relocating past them.

Point

And certainly, every wonderful tactical story, especially those shared in a work environment scenario, has an indication. There is a vital message, discovering or takeaway that the target market attracts from the story you've just informed: one that normally flows from the plot of your story as well as its impact on the individual in it. Due to the fact that having a strength is main to my story's success, I normally do not like to leave its communication to opportunity as well as will certainly commonly conclude my tale by driving the factor home-- e.g. "The point of this story is ..." or "What I gained from that circumstance was ..." or "The factor I shared this story with you is ...".

ELEMENTS OF STORYTELLING

In the business world, narration can be specified as an organisation, large or small, using specialist and in some cases personal tales to supply info about you, your objective, and your services or items to the globe. What are your service accomplishments skillfully and/or within your greater community?

An organisation with a great story will have customers that trust them and are loyal to the brand, as well as higher brand name identification. With motifs, brilliant messages, unforgettable characters and an interesting story that every person can associate with, companies have actually had the ability to release their companies using indigenous storytelling.

Telling your firm tale is essential, and company storytelling is as much of an art form as writing a novel. Yes, a PR business can aid, but in order to be efficient AS a tale, it requires to be informed as well as re-told, which means everybody has to be willing as well as able to tell the story.

However, there's no universal formula. What I've observed in the past is that in times of problem, or failing, individuals are really quick to blame their tools. In this case, the 'devices' are the building blocks of the tale.

We fail to remember that those foundations aren't the issue-- it's what we make with those blocks. A tale is a lot more than just a couple of realities or occasions. A story is a complete image; the way those occasions are connected.

The 'Hunter and a Bear' video clips are the best examples of a business bringing itself back from a decline in the electronic period. To cut a long story short, it was an excellent usage of a narrative.

It would be naïve to presume that a narrow interpretation of what makes story goodwill certainly help us to come to be better authors. These components can be blended, matched and used in a range of means depending on the context in which the story is informed, and also its purpose.

1.   Message

Narration as a branding tool is not regarding telling tales just for the sake of it. Rather, for many marketers, the narration is about making use of stories to interact with messages that reflect positively on the brand. But initially, you must develop a clearly defined message. Without it, there is no factor to tell stories-- a minimum of not with a tactical purpose.

2. Conflict

Conflict is the driving force of a good tale. No conflict, no story.But why is this the instance? The response hinges on human nature. As humans, we naturally seek equilibrium as well as harmony in our lives. As quickly as consistency is disrupted, we do whatever we can to restore it. When confronted with a problem-- a dispute-- we instinctively seek to discover a solution. Problem forces us to act. As writers, we get our message throughout with conflict as well as its resolution. The problem in your service tale may be the obstacles your consumers are experiencing that you assist them in conquering. It may be a company difficulty that you encountered as an organization that shaped you right into being what you are today. As you consider these hardships, you'll be able to discover a couple of that have a crucial function in your tale.

3. Characters

Another basic component is your personalities. We have seen how dispute notes the turning point in the story, however in order for this problem to play out, you require a cast of interacting and compelling characters. So as to get personally included with a story, we need to be able to understand the characters. Here it is essential to maintain your target market in mind. The target market needs to be able to understand both the problem and the hero. Based upon our requirement to have equilibrium in our lives, we will generally emphasize with a person faced with a conflict.

4.   Plot

The flow of the tale, as well as its events, are important to the audience's experience. Provided the reality that we can just tell one point at a time, and that a tale exists just as a progression of events within a provided time period, the series of events requires careful consideration.

5. Get emotional

Determine the type of feelings you 'd ideally like your target market to really feel, and craft your story to strike those notes. Please don't hesitate to share what's true as well as real to you.A wonderful story evokes a psychological response. Audiences need to really feel something as you share your story. This will certainly originate from the methods which you combine your tale components to reveal that you are at the core of your company and also what you have experienced to obtain where you are and to assist those that you offer.
, if you have no feeling telling your story-- the audience won't really feel feeling either.

5.   **Engaging**

In telling your story-- reveal it! Use words that will certainly enable the audience to picture what you're saying, words that will make the listener part of the experience as well as part of you. This develops a psychological connection with the listener.

6.   **Personalized with Audio and Visuals**

When telling your story with a device like a video clip, it is powerful to supplement your tale with music and visuals. These can assist tell your story. They assist set the stage. They present the characters. They can emphasize the dispute.

They assist stimulate and engage feeling. Video advertising is a powerful way to tell your story. Do not forget these powerful devices.

7.   **Short in Length**

You desire to be able to inform your organisation tale in a means that captures interest and also after that holds it without shedding it. Your story can differ depending on where you're informing it. Of course, you can inform your story in a lengthier means in other areas. However, you desire to be able to record the fundamentals in as little time as required.

TELLING STORIES WITH DATA

Any type of fantastic tale means visualization and also information. It takes the tiny enhancements of those details to build an image in a person's mind to absolutely make the tale full. The same goes for analytics and information. These additions to our advertising and marketing techniques make it so that as online marketers, we can inform the stories that produce successful projects and also customer trips. Nevertheless, translating all the data correctly and also transforming it into a great story can be an intimidating task that several organizations have a hard time to achieve.

It is the fiction that makes fantastic books and also motion pictures. All of these types of storytelling are spoken-- either spoken or created words. We do not commonly assume data or factual details as informing tales. However, it surely does. There is a story in every chunk of data that is depicted in a graph, a graph, a representation, a scatter plot, or some kind of metaphoric illustration, such as a pyramid.

There are few methods much more prominent in a presentation than referencing raw data. Having the capability to share finished research study or the analysis of gathered data offers the subject you are presenting on the needed context as well as valid basis that we as human beings require in order to approve something like reality.

With analytical devices and abilities, people in these very technological positions have the ability to sort through the massive amounts of information being collected in order to determine trends, assess findings, as well as draw conclusions from the data that other business groups can reference when choosing.

I would include that a superb visualization additionally informs a tale through the visual depiction of statistical details. To this end, the visualization needs to tell a tale to the audience. Storytelling aids the viewer to gain insight from the data.

Brand name storytelling would be much more interesting if marketing professionals believed more like journalists, who make use of publicly available information to give brand-new angles and insights to things that influence people's lives.

By utilizing data, which people consider reliable, in your tales, it makes your brand name a lot more legitimate to readers.

Basic Steps to Telling a Story With Data

Here are some strategies on telling a good story that apply to data visualizations.

1. Find a compelling narrative.

If you do not, then maybe this visualization should support exploratory information analysis (EDA) instead than convey info. For the developer of an exploratory visualization, it is still essential to trigger the customers' imagination to motivate taking a look at partnerships among as well as assist in connecting with the data-- assume gamification.

2. Think about your audience.

Another helpful tactic for assisting translate chilly, difficult information right into something that your audience can spend in is to assume through exactly how this information associates to your particular audience. Taking the time to connect to your target market in this method will go a lengthy way in making your presentation impactful. The visualization needs to be framed around the level of information the audience already has, wrong and also appropriate:

- **Novice:** initially direct exposure to the topic, yet does not desire oversimplification
- **Generalist:** aware of the subject, but trying to find an overview understanding and significant themes
- **Managerial:** extensive, workable understanding of intricacies as well as correlations with accessibility to detail
- **Expert**: extra exploration and also exploration and much less narration with excellent detail
- **Executive:** just has time to amass the value as well as conclusions of heavy possibilities

3. Don't Censor.

Don't be discerning regarding the data you omit or include, unless you're positive you're offering your audience the most effective representation of what the information "claims". This selectivity includes making use of discrete values when the information is continual; how you manage missing, outlier as well as out of array values; approximate temporal arrays; capped worths, quantities, ranges, and also intervals. Customers will at some point figure that out as well as shed count on the visualization (and any others you could generate).

4. Stick to a Linear Timeline

There have actually been some really favoured tales told through recalls or timelines that jump between previous, existing, and future, the most frequently effective narratives are ones that are told in a clear beginning, centre, and also end order.It can be alluring to begin a data analysis discussion off by describing your findings, specifically after investing so much time working through disorganized information in order to draw such verdicts. Nonetheless, diving right into a checklist of facts as well as numbers without the correct history info can be alienating to those that don't have the required context to see its worth. Instead, take some time to lay the groundwork of your 'tale' by reviewing the trouble the organization was attempting to fix with this data analysis. Remind your audience of why you're all below, what they'll be becoming aware of, and why it matters.

COMPLEX BUT CLEAR

It seems all too obvious: Only clear communication can inform and convince an audience. Harry Truman's stating that "if you can not convince them, perplex them" no longer works with today's wise and linked public. If people do not recognize a news release, a financier discussion, an email message or a customer letter, they merely neglect it as well as rely on various other resources. As a result, we as communicators typically don't even recognize that our interaction has been vague.

What is clear to us may be confusing to our target market. Just how can such complex subjects be made clear without oversimplifying the message?

A brand-new study by the University of St. Gallen, "Complex to Clear," addresses these questions. Its major facility is that achieving clear interaction calls for greater than simply cleaning up on your composing abilities. It calls for an organized management initiative. The research puts together tried and tested techniques as well as tools, interesting case studies, as well as the results from three surveys with greater than 460 skilled communicators from worldwide.

Complex topics

What makes a topic a complex one? Primarily, four qualities make a message tough to recognize:

1. A great variety of pertinent elements, items or elements.

2. Several partnerships among these aspects.

3. Numerous modifications in these relationships in time.

4. A lack of introduction regarding these relationships and also their modifications.

Facility subjects contain many elements that communicate in a dynamic, murky and also multilateral manner. Case in points of this is messages about service approach, the causes of a crisis, or the components of a brand-new product, service or organisation design.

To clear up something complicated, you must structure (or team) products to reduce their number, focus on their essential partnerships, and offer an overview before going into detail, while likewise thinking about the changes that may take place after your communication has happened. Due to this last component, it is necessary to contextualize messages in terms of their day, purpose as well as scope.

How To Be Clear

The research identified five aspects that distinguish a clear message from a complicated one: A clear message includes simply adequate background information to recognize its context or why (and also by whom) is a must-read. A clear message is rationally structured as well as reduced to its necessary aspects. A clear message is devoid of uncertain terms as well as includes stimulating elements that reverberate with its target market. (See the chart on web page 35 to figure out whether a certain message satisfies the criteria for CLEAR interaction.).

Organizations that wish to attend to clarity as a critical possession must also think of organizational measures for clear communication.

Relocating from facility to clear messages in a constant, lasting way needs a number of business activities that can be summed up in the STARTER phrase (see chart below). The components in this acronym (criteria, training, accountability, evaluation, tools, examples, resources) ensure that different business levers are made use of to institutionalize clear interaction in a business.

First, the company must specify standards pertaining to clear communication. This indicates it has to explicitly define high-quality standards for its external as well as internal communication (as well as exactly how these criteria can be fulfilled). The value of "solution," as an example, requires staff members to write in short and also succinct sentences in a pleasant design, concentrating on the appropriate and utilizing just usual terms.

BASIC THINGS STORYTELLING CAN DO FOR YOU

It's been called one of the most valuable organisation skill of the next decade. A scientifically-proven method to intrigue target markets and also obtain them to do what you want.

However, if you point out storytelling to some local business owner or advertising supervisors, you'll often get an empty look in return. Perhaps even a frown.

There are a couple of possible reasons:

When much of us consider narration, we believe motion pictures, books, and huge budget commercials jobs that need large spending plans and big ad agencies and conference rooms loaded with "skill." It looks like something that's out of reach for small firms. However, the narration is actually one of the least expensive advertising and marketing methods. You've already got the costly tools: your brain. That is the story generator. A blog, or a video camera, or perhaps pastels are all you need to communicate it.

Storytelling can seem like simply another advertising and marketing craze up until you've gotten the appropriate intro to it. Due to the fact that storytelling is actually the earliest advertising method ever before.

You know the story of Adam and Eve, right? Well, let's sight that as an advertising and marketing story. The message (this is a dumbed-down version of the story, as I am not a Bible scholar) is to follow God or poor points will certainly occur.

You might strongly differ with my interpretation of that messaging, but there's no chance around it: That story sends out a message regarding exactly how we need to act. It intends to convince us to act in a specific method, though it does not overly appear and tell us so. Yet boy, do we obtain the message anyhow.

Do you see the similarities between this as well as advertising and marketing? Advertising and marketing are, eventually, regarding supplying a convincing message. Stories are a wonderful method to do that.

Equipped with that said details, a lot of local business owner is much more responsive to trying some storytelling.

Exactly how, exactly? Should they burst out the fountain and the parchment pen, as well as begin with "A long time ago? No.

They should try a few things like this:

1. Tell the story of how you started your business.

Allow's begin with the easy things first. Every service has some sort of a tale about how it happened. These are called "origin tales" worldwide of filmmaking as well as books. Some beginning tales are much more interesting than others-- think "Batman Begins" versus "How ABC Accounting Was Founded." Both of those are beginning tales.

It's not a bad start. However, there's even more that could be done here. For example, a brief two- or three-minute video of the owner discussing exactly how the company became might be even more engaging than this. It would certainly offer the company a human face, for beginners, and would let the audience vicariously share in the enjoyment and anxiousness that goes along with introducing a new organisation.

That would certainly offer audiences a means to share the founder's experience, which is an effective and also engaging approach. This is the very acme of storytelling-- to let others share in our experiences.

It transforms out that when we hear an excellent tale, we live it for ourselves to a specific degree. Our audiences recognize with us much better after they've listened to the tale.

While video clips are ideal for narration, if you can't get your creator before a camera, there are a lot of other options. Attempt to get some photographs that represent the business's start. Even a picture of the proverbial garage or your house which contained the first home office will do.

2. Share your customers' stories

These are, certainly, known as case studies. They're real-world instances of exactly how your services or products have profited genuine consumers.

Study are exceptionally reliable. It's time to obtain some if you don't have a couple of in your content toolbox currently.

Create a list of 3-7 customers or consumers who've gotten especially excellent results from collaborating with you. These ought to be individuals you've nearly come to be close friends with-- clients that are satisfied and also probably eager to aid you out.

Consider what kind of settlement you may give them for helping with the study. Often, it doesn't have to be anything. Other times, a discount rate could be suitable, or perhaps accessibility to a unique product or attribute you understand they're interested in yet aren't fairly all set to pay for.

Attempt to prevent straight money settlements. They often tend to lead to case studies that appear stilted, and also the company giving the study might feel in a different way toward you afterwards.

If you do a great deal of promo of the study, the exposure for their brand name could be sufficient to persuade your companion company to do the study for no "settlement" ... though they're generally taking payment in the complimentary advertising, they'll receive from taking part.

Get really details about what you desire the case study to cover. Generally, they're about 2-3 pages long, perhaps 500 to 1,000 words. You'll want to access the very least 3-4 straight quotes from the customer, so you'll need to do an interview. You may also want to obtain records or some visual data that shows the before-and-after story of how you helped them. You'll also need a number of photos of the firm and of its workers.

If the information you'll be obtaining from the business might be taken into consideration personal, think about hiding the identity of the business. This is much less than excellent. However, several companies are really protective of their information as well as inside processes. They might not agree to do the case study unless they can secure company keys.

Provide the firm with a chance to review (as well as have the choice to make adjustments to) the case study prior to it gets published. You do not want any type of shocks as well as you certainly don't wish to make them unhappy.

3. Share customer experiences on social media.

User-generated content is among the most interesting things in marketing right now. It's trusted greater than brand-created web content and is typically even more reliable at creating sales than brand-created web content.

The user-generated content you'll get possibly will not be a typical, totally fleshed out story, with a start as well as a centre and also an end. What you'll get will certainly resemble a frame of a flick instead. Yet it's enough-- we people are wonderful at filling out missing out on info concerning other individuals' tales (almost to a fault).

4. Share stories of your employees or of your company culture.

"People associate with people." You've heard it a thousand times. Below's exactly how to use it: Use the tales of exactly how you operate to reveal your firm society.

This is much more efficient than just declaring you uphold particular features. So rather than saying "We motivate our employees to take risks," tell the stories of exactly how employees took threats.

You can likewise tell stories concerning your own staff members. When Karrie Sundbom (our Content Marketing Manager) joined Act-On, we published an article regarding her background and also why she came to function here. You could do this for virtually any type of staff member if your business is little, or simply for senior personnel if you're mid-sized.

Bonus offer benefit: These kinds of firm stories are excellent for attracting prospective hires. The more you can share regarding what it's like to work at your business, the much better. It will assist you in bringing in individuals who would certainly be an excellent fit, and also can likewise help individuals that won't be an excellent fit to know that at an early stage. Both things conserve HR a lot of time.

5. Write better press releases.

Desire some cost-free media exposure? That does not? And yet, many press releases have to do with as compelling as cardboard.

So turn it around. Make your business's newest item launch, or brand-new area, or whatever, right into a tale.

If it's a brand-new executive's task), there's always an angle for these points there's constantly some catalyst (also. Inform that tale. Include a couple of details regarding the important players who made it occur. Sprinkle in a bit regarding what difficulties they faced. Share some specifics regarding essential turning points or developments of the job.

Journalists and also editors are far more likely to reply to information like that. Particularly if you recommend your business's certain story might connect right into, state, the motif of an American company. Or the theme of creative use of sources or nearly anything else.

USE OWN STORIES TO BUILD CREDIBILITY

When you introduce your business, as an example, do not tell your prospects you can save them 10% on their telecommunications expenses, or that you've collaborated with the leading cars and truck manufacturers. Obtain that same message throughout in an individual tale as well as it will have so much extra power. Admittedly, the second intro is a couple of sentences much longer-- yet those added sentences-- and also the method the whole introduction is worded-- make a world of difference. Think regarding just how you would respond to the introductions as the CEO of a Packaging company.

Let's talk about three strategies for building sales-driving credibility into your copy.

1. The "about me" approach

This is most likely one of the most recognizable credibility-building tools, due to the fact that you see it almost everywhere.

You can additionally make use of a bit extra nuance when introducing yourself to your buyers.

Utilizing a "Why I created this item" technique, you can weave your own tale right into your sales material, by incorporating details about your experience and credentials with benefit-driven copy that decreases your viewers' resistance to buying.Explain what you're providing for clients, how your approach addresses the outcomes you deliver to those clients, and then segue right into your sales message.

2. The "reluctant hero" approach

One more approach is the tale of the "unintentional item." This works by setting up a backstory where the item producer starts acquiring credibility for producing results, and then other individuals begin demanding to recognize just how to make it happen for themselves.The unwilling hero is a storytelling archetype, as well as you may think that makes this approach standard or contrived. But assuming your tale is both true and compelling (yes, it requires to be both), the reluctant hero tale is an extremely reliable integrity generator.

3. The customer-as-proof approach

A 3rd (and extremely effective) technique is to make effective customers the focus of your credibility-building story. After all, why talk about yourself when you can talk regarding the sensational outcomes your consumers have developed and produce integrity by association? When the instance is piled upon example, the feeling of integrity is continuously heightened.

STORY HOOKS

The business world could appear buttoned-down from the outdoors - yet actually, it's a whole lot extra intriguing than you may understand. Numerous business owners are understood for being vibrant characters, both at the office and also in their personal lives. Nevertheless, following rules and also staying inside the lines does not typically make for company success! From winning seed money in an online poker video game to trying to duplicate dinosaurs.

Here are things that entrepreneurs should know about writing a good story.

1. Set the Scene & Introduce the Hero

A blunder several companies make-believes they're the hero in their success stories. The real hero should always be your customer, not you. And that's why you ought to start your success tales with an introductory right into your client.

2. Make Your Audience Hate the Villain

Be certain to use actual reviews in this area, even if you do not utilize them anywhere else in the case study. Tease out your client's pain factor as well as utilize the language they make use of to describe just how it influenced them.

3. Bring in the Ally Who Saves the Day

It's time for the remedy to your client's problem. At this phase, you add yourself to the success tale and discuss exactly how you resolved the core issue. Remember, you're the ally that aids the hero beat their adversaries. Just make sure you return to exactly how your item or solution resolved their trouble and the procedure they went via to apply it.

4. Celebrate the Happy Ending

This is where your information all the good points that took place thanks to the service as well as wrap up the story.Include as numerous information as feasible at this stage. Whether they're quantitative or qualitative, be certain to consist of them.How did things get far better for your customer after they utilized your product or solution? Make your audience really care by grounding these points in the vital objectives as well as worths you developed previously in the success story.

THE SECRET STRATEGY THAT MASTER STORYTELLERS USE.

Absolutely nothing keeps a person on the edge of their seat like a good story. That's why people love to enjoy motion pictures, read publications, and binge-watch television shows. I recognize all of us have that a person good friend or member of the family that informs the most effective tales around the table. What if there was a method to turn those stories into dollars? There is. If you can get customers to link with your stories, you'll be able to boost your sales. Several of you might be believing, "I'm a terrible storyteller, so this won't work for me."And several of you might claim, "My life is tiring. I don't have any type of excellent tales to tell." Yes, storytelling is an art. Not everyone is born with the capability to tell an engaging story. Thankfully for you, I'm extremely familiar with narration.

I use this approach all the time as a marketing technique.In advertising, effective storytelling is all about the transformation that your item will bring to its consumers. While we all know stories need to have a start, middle and also end , it's not in fact that beneficial to think of them in stop similarly when it comes to marketing.Consider this: if you're adhering to the common beginning-middle-end design, you might make a story about your sandwich organisation as an example that goes something like, "Jordan neglected he had a sandwich in his layer pocket, he got to in, he got the sandwich, he begins eating it, and also completes consuming the sandwich. Acquire sandwiches at Jordan's sandwich store".

1. Immerse your audience in a story.

A well-told tale is something that will embed your audience's mind for years to come. A well-told tale is something that will certainly embed your audience's mind for years to come. Take this simple yet remarkable TED talk as an example. In it, a 12-year-old Masai child from Kenya called Richard Turere moves his audience to one more world by narrating regarding his experiences in his homeland. With basic words and also slides with big, graphic images, Richard weaves an exciting story of exactly how he created a system of lights that had the ability to protect his household's animals from lion attacks. The reason this presentation was so effective was that every word and picture presented helped to produce a clear psychological photo of the problem Richard as well as his family members faced. Also, it plainly followed a principle of presentation-giving, which is to utilize visuals that supplement your tale instead of repeat what has actually currently been said.Another method to engage the audience in your story is to provide sensory details that will certainly allow them to in fact see, listen to, really feel, as well as smell the different stimulations in your story world. According to AkashKaria, this will certainly turn the discussion right into a mental motion picture that the target market can not aid yet engage in, as is performed in this TED talk.Unlike books, however, presentations must use brief, however efficient descriptions.

2. Tell a personal story.

Few things are as exciting as a personal story, especially those of victory over severe adversity.In his informative book The Seven Basic Plots, author Christopher Booker discovers that there are 7 basic tale plots that have universal appeal. These include the tale of the hero defeating a beast, the rags-to-riches tale, the quest for a prize, as well as the voyage of a hero who returns a transformed person. These plots are plainly seen in a few of one of the most prominent as well as moving presentations ever offered. Take, for instance, this harrowing and also gripping tale of a woman's escape from her homeland of North Korea. Or this woman's the similarly powerful story of residential physical violence and also how she located the courage to leave her violent spouse.

3. Create suspense.

Those that love to watch films or review books recognize that a good story constantly needs to have a problem and also a plot. These 2 aspects are what make a good discussion right into a roller rollercoaster flight that maintains listeners/viewers at the edge of their seats, asking themselves, "What will take place next?" There are several gadgets that can increase the level of the thriller of your tale. One way is to narrate chronologically and also accumulate to a climactic conclusion, as is done right here in this tale about a lady that was birthed without fibula bones and also grew up to be an established professional athlete, starlet as well as model. One more way is to plop the viewer/listener right in the centre of activity and afterwards go backwards in time to disclose how every one of this occurred. A good example of this is Zak Ibrahim's tale, which starts with the revelation that his daddy was involved in the World Trade Center bombing. He after that goes back in time to inform occasions from his youth and also just how he matured to select a various course from his dad's. A third means is to begin by informing a predictable tale and then shock the target market by taking a totally different turn from what was expected. This TED talk begins with a presenter that leads his audience to believe he doesn't talk English, just to surprise them in order to make a point concerning just how we create identity.

4. Bring characters to life.

Characters are at the heart of any tale. Their bad luck, as well as fortunes, are what make individuals want to laugh, cry or celebrate. The most successful stories, I found, were those that developed three-dimensional personalities who were simple to recognize as well as, at the very same time, had an unusual attribute. In order to do this, you should provide sufficient information to bring the character to life in the minds of those in the target market. Master writer Malcolm Gladwell produces a dazzling image of Howard in this presentation by defining his physical look and mentioning his leisure activities as well as obsessions.

5. Show. Don't tell.

Instead of informing your audience about a specific event in a story, attempt revealing them by moving them to a scene. In the introduction to this chapter, I could have simply informed you that I had a shy schoolmate who one day wowed the entire course with an incredible discussion. This, nevertheless, would certainly not have had the very same result as utilizing summaries of setting as well as conversations to take you to the centre of a scene. So, whenever you supply a story, attempt scene-by-scene building and construction of occasions and also make use of dialogue instead of narrative, as seen in this presentation which won the 2014 World Championship of Public Speaking.

HOW TO ENGAGE YOUR AUDIENCE

There are a lot of myths out there when it comes to involving an audience. Several presenters have been informed that the trick to keeping an audience's interest is the charm. Appeal and confidence are fantastic assets to presenters. However, you don't need to be Steve Jobs to get your audience's interest. The real trick to engaging your audience is something you do before you march to offer. It's something you do before you begin practising. It's something you do prior to you also produce your slides. Understanding exactly how to structure your presentation is where involving your audience actually starts.

Develop a Winning Structure

When it comes to structuring your message, Empathy is extremely beneficial. Resist the lure to use your presentation as a platform to display all your new products' cool brand-new features or all the excellent comments you've had from previous clients. Though it is important to highlight your toughness, it is more vital to satisfy your audience's requirements. Do your study. Learn what challenges your audience is attempting to get rid of or what they want. You can then structure your arguments around these requirements, straight addressing your audience's needs, interests, as well as issues. At this moment comes the lure to chuck in a whole number of fantastic data, beautiful responses, checklists of fancy features, and extra capacities. Withstand! Including a bunch of weak arguments will decrease the total stamina of your message. If you provide a couple of solid disagreements, the effect of your discussion will be much greater.

Start Negative, End Positive

It may break all our instincts, but there is no better method to get people to sit up and also listen than speaking about their problems. You can be going over a problem they are already aware of, in which case you are again using empathy to address their requirements. You could additionally be showing them a problem they haven't also thought about yet. This puts you in an excellent position to let your experience sparkle and also provide your audience with details of real value. After this adverse beginning, you need to lead the audience with your method to the problem. Address the concerns that you've brought up by detailing those strong arguments for your service. Finish the presentation by looking in the direction of a future where-- with your aid-- the problem has relapsed, and also they are better off. By taking them on this journey from adverse to favourable, they will clearly comprehend just how they can benefit from collaborating with you. Empathizing (yeah, that old chestnut) with your audience's difficulties and also issues isn't specifically a sales tool. You can use this in any type of discussion to catch your target market's imagination as well as illustrate the importance of listening very carefully to what you have to state.

Use Audience-First Language

After you've structured your presentation, you could want to create a script or some audio speaker notes. When producing your talking notes, constantly keep your audience at the front of your mind. Take them along for the flight by using language that centres around them: great deals extra "you," "your requirements," "your success" as well as a little bit much less "us," "our customers," "our item." By framing your entire narrative around the audience's wants and also requires, you quickly connect with them and keep them engaged. And because you've been focusing on the target market from stage one, this should be rather very easy to attain.

Master Your Notes

Robotically reading from notes is a fantastic method to get your target market to nod off. Instead, dedicate your key points to memory as well as exercise your shipment while clicking through your slides. A well-rehearsed presentation always seems more natural. Your target market will certainly really feel that they are being talked to, not chatted at. It is likewise crucial to recognize your web content well enough to readjust in the situation of emergency. Does an emergency alarm cut your hour-long presentation down to 30 mins? Well, if you know your story as well as your material, you'll be able to pick out the most important information and also still wow your target market.

The concept behind effective involvement, those that have been involved in this effort state, is this: Whatever you do, see to it the members of an area recognize you value them-- both by treating them with respect and also by showing them that together, they have crucial things to teach each other.Seize the chances to join people around their interests, nevertheless, and you'll discover that your efforts to engage these neighbourhoods will get simpler as well as more efficient. Because of the optimal scenario, the engagement procedure ends up being a cycle. One that expands stronger with each iteration, and wants to establish links with the target market not just for the purpose of the existing task, however, for all the tasks still in advance.

These are some ways to engage your customers through social media

1. Make your content unique and engaging

Your content will simply fade right into the background chatter of social media if you're not composing something that your audience can not get anywhere else. You can become a professional in your certain company particular niche by offering up insightful details that your target market regards important. When your clients and leads know and also trust you and like what you have to claim, they're likely to share your web content with their friends.

2. Use strong headlines and accessible prose

A good headline tempts your readers to click on a link and needs to contain adequate information to gauge what it is they're clicking. Fill your headings with action verbs and keywords. Beyond the headline, make sure your writing comes. Do not use industry jargon or attempt to appear clever by describing something in a needlessly complex method.

3. Offer up differed, multimedia material

Web content can and must take several forms, from blog messages and white papers to infographics as well as slideshows and videos. Each system supplies a different way to existing info, and also as you check out these various systems, you'll get a sense of what tools resonate with your target market. The key is to keep things fresh with a selection of media that will certainly thrill, shock, amuse and also educate your target market.

It is so crucial to track your audiences' chatter on social media, to pay interest to what's trending and also what's getting your target market aggravated or ecstatic or curious. When you can maintain your pulse on the social media conversation, you can customize as well as adjust your web content in means that will certainly really feel fresh as well as allure to the perceptiveness as well as passions of your target market.

5. Track when your target market is most energetic

Use social media analytics to track when your audience is interacting with your content. Let's claim you figure out that the majority of your audience is retweeting and also "taste" your material on a weekday early mornings-- if that's the case, dish out your finest stuff on weekday mornings. The goal is to cater to the days and also times of day when the largest part of your audience is involving as well as clicking your content.

6. Create motivations for sharing

Like any target market, your social networks target market likes chances and giveaways to gain something for nothing. There's absolutely nothing wrong with incentivizing your target market to retweet and also share your blog posts by providing something back. Probably you could be entering them right into a competition to win a tiny prize, or maybe you could be giving them a price cut on one of your preferred service or products.

Steps To A Much Better Discussion

Many service connections have unmentioned policies with assumptions at their core. This might function for a while, but it's better for all sides to communicate expectations as well as needs freely. Efficient organisation communication can bring favourable modification, even if points have been bad.

Discover a great place and also time for all included to chat.

Communication won't work when one event is distracted. Locate a silent area and, if the interaction is difficult, see to it you have personal privacy. Have regular frameworks such as weekly or regular monthly meetings to sustain communication, as well as make time to talk when there's an issue to solve.

To be listened to, pay attention initially.

The greatest company interaction awesome is failing to listen. To listen as well as after that, enforce your recommended solution is not paying attention. Paying attention sends out the best message of all: We're working to find a mutually appropriate remedy.

Ask inquiries

These assist you to obtain comments, show that you're listening, validate understanding and also offer regard. Questions are wonderful tools and also must be made use of usually. If you're not sure regarding a detail, ask for verification. Just ask if you desire to hear comments from the various other individuals. You've opened up effective two-way company communication when you incorporate paying attention by asking pertinent inquiries.

Revealing feeling is necessary, yet constantly be considerate.

It's flawlessly acceptable to tell someone, "When you do not join in to help the team, it frustrates me." Yet you need to additionally anticipate your co-worker to say something like, "It upsets me when I have way too much work." That's a penalty. What you require to do is find a means to fix the problem. You might start by equally clearing up occupational assumptions. Feeling belongs to that interaction. However, it should not be the end of it.

Pay attention to nonverbal messages.

It's tough to have open communication if both sides fold their arms, clench their jaws as well as refuse to look at each other in the eye. Below, the nonverbal signals are screaming even if words aren't. Beware regarding your tone of voice, too. It may be better to wait up until points resolve if nonverbal messages are frustrating the discussion. Nod your head and also maintain an open pose to show you're absorbing what the various other individual is claiming.

Acknowledge and enhance positive actions.

Efficient communication is a continuous task, and also you should say thanks to the other person for suiting you. This is a win-win, as well as it will certainly maintain the channels of interaction open.

Hold your horses and also don't anticipate wonders. Communication is so essential and so hard. Eventually, good organisation interaction is not regarding winning; it's about reinforcing relationships.

CONCLUSION

Organisation communication is utilized to promote a product, organization, or service ; relay info within a company; or deal with legal and also comparable concerns. Business communication might likewise refer to interior interaction: a communications supervisor will usually handle inner communication and also craft messages sent out to employees.

Failings of human interaction can end up being magnified in professional settings. In service deals, especially those involving large quantities of money, a little miscommunication can have terrible effects. Because of this, clarity is absolutely important. Interaction has to correspond, concise, as well as straightforward in order to make sure the desired message is received.

The objective of public relationships is to share details regarding a company. These details can be ahead of upcoming events or product launches, or to quell reports or stop the spread of incorrect info about a company. Public relations likewise entails proactively informing team on replying to media so wrong info is not released in the first place.

Numerous small businesses and also start-ups lack big advertising and marketing budgets; they depend on public relationships to build a "buzz" regarding a future company or item launch. One goal of a public relationships campaign is to produce editorial coverage for service since content coverage is viewed as more genuine than advertising and marketing.

Do Not Go Yet; One Last Thing To Do

If you enjoyed this book or found it useful, I'd be very grateful if you'd post a short review on Amazon. Your support really does make a difference, and I read all the reviews personally so I can get your feedback and make this book even better.

Thanks again for your support!

www.ingramcontent.com/pod-product-compliance
Lightning Source LLC
Chambersburg PA
CBHW070828220526
45466CB00002B/772